Write What You Think!

Carson-Dellosa Publishing Company, Inc.
Greensboro, North Carolina

Dedication

A special thanks to all of the children who have shared their personal writing with me throughout the years.

Also, thanks to my friends whom I value and appreciate more than words can express.

To my parents who have always believed in me and supported my dreams.

Especially to my children:
McKenzie—my darling daughter who brightens my world with her love and energy!

Zach—my amazing son who inspires me with his compassion and zest for life!

—Cyndi Walters

Prompts Contributed By: Cyndi Walters
Editor: Kelly Gunzenhauser
Layout Design: Van Harris
Artists: Bill Neville & Van Harris
Cover Design: Peggy Jackson

Table of Contents

Introduction

Despite the growing emphasis on process writing and student topic generation, most students are still tested on how they write to prompts and need to practice responding to prompts. Many students have difficulty responding well, partly because they do not feel invested in this type of writing. However, there are ways to help students see that writing to prompts is fun.

Read, Think, and Respond

The prompts in this book are meant to challenge students to tap into their thoughts and feelings, and then respond to those thoughts and feelings in writing. Students will find that brief paragraph answers may suffice for some of the prompts, while other prompts may inspire them to pour their hearts out on paper.

Prompt Categories

All About Me: These are good prompts to begin with because most students enjoy talking and writing about themselves and their opinions. With these prompts, you can often get students to open up, either in discussion or on paper. Some of these require simple answers, while others require more thought.

Family Relationships: This category can be great inspiration for discussion or writing, but requires sensitivity when choosing prompts. Remember that there are many different kinds of families. Before you assign these prompts, consider students' situations. Change wording, if necessary, or offer a choice of prompts.

Friendships: Most of these prompts are designed to have students consider the general state of friendship, but some deal with specific situations. Many of these are ideal for use at the beginning of the year, in order to lead students toward being kind to each other.

School: Many triumphs, joys, and conflicts happen during school. By choosing from the prompts below, you can find out how to solve class conflicts, learn about students' interests and talents, and even get an impromptu teaching evaluation.

Academics: Opportunities for using academic writing prompts often present themselves during the school day. These can be used in addition to specific, curriculum-based prompts.

Character Education and Safety: Use these prompts to address specific topics, such as behavior, peer pressure, honesty, and perseverance.

Points to Ponder/Problem Solving: In this category, prompts ask students for their opinions about a wide variety of things, from being a leader to participating in co-ed sports to becoming grown-ups. Many of these are "What if" types of questions, which students seem to love to ask as well as answer!

Story/Fiction Narrative: These require more imagination and less introspection than the prompts in the other categories. Use these to give students a chance to stretch their creative writing wings, take a break from expository writing, or prepare for tests that have narrative writing prompts.

Other Suggestions for Using Prompts

There are several ways to distribute and use prompts. Some suggestions for using them to inspire class discussions or writing are:

- Use the traditional method: assign a single prompt and ask students to respond in writing.

- Copy and cut apart the prompts. Place them in a jar in your writing center and let students choose prompts from the jar to discuss (or to respond to during writing time).

- Post a few prompts on the board or in the center and let students vote on which one to discuss, or allow each student to choose one to write about.

- Have students modify a prompt by changing genres and audiences. For example, a response to the prompt "If you could choose your family's dessert tonight, what would it be?" could turn into a shopping list and recipe for parents, telling how the student thinks the dessert is made.

- Reward a student by letting her look through the book and select a few prompts to post on the board for her classmates to choose from.

- Have students take their best responses through the writing process. Publish the final pieces.

Teaching Tips for Successfully Working with Prompts

The following suggestions will help you keep the activity of writing to prompts as enjoyable as possible for students.

- Begin by using the prompts for discussions to introduce students to the nature of a prompt question and to expose them to their classmates' differing answers. Hearing other answers helps students consider more possibilities as they write.

- When selecting prompts, be sensitive and use common sense. Reword prompts as needed. For example, since many children do not have intact families, serious conflicts between students can occasionally arise. Alter prompts, if needed, to suit these situations. You know your students best, so use that knowledge to make good prompt choices.

- Set guidelines for how students should treat each other during discussions. Students should be respectful of each other and must agree to disagree about some issues. When students review each other's writing, they should transfer this respectful behavior to their comments.

- After revealing a prompt, have a class discussion. Then, let students write. Discussion can be the brainstorming step in the writing process. During the discussion, students can sort through their thoughts and jot down notes as they listen to classmates' comments.

- Let students further invest themselves in writing by having them write and submit their own prompts. Occasionally choose a student's prompt to assign. Always screen prompts ahead of time for appropriate content.

- Show students how to move from either short answers or lists to paragraphs, full essays, and stories. For example, demonstrate different responses a student can have to the prompt "What is your favorite kind of cake? Why?"

  Response #1 (Short answer):
  My favorite kind of cake is yellow cake with chocolate frosting because it tastes good.

  Response #2 (Paragraph):
  I love all kinds of cake, but my favorite is yellow cake with chocolate icing. Yellow cake without chocolate icing is good if that is the only kind you have, but it is not my first choice. I love chocolate and candy, so I tried chocolate cake with chocolate icing, but that made me feel sick, and I was too hyper afterwards. Then, I tried yellow cake with chocolate icing. The icing tasted like candy but wasn't too heavy. So for now, that's my favorite.

All About Me

Think about a time in your life when something unexpected happened. What happened? How did you feel?

Think about your favorite holiday. Describe this holiday through each of your five senses. What do you see, hear, feel, smell, and taste?

Your parent has just told you that your little brother or sister will have to share your bedroom. Write a letter persuading your parent why you feel this is not a good idea.

Who is your best friend? Write a letter to your friend that explains why your friendship is so important.

Imagine your neighbor is going to take care of your pet while you are away. Write your neighbor to explain how to care for your pet.

All About Me

What do you like to write about and why?

Describe the very first memory that you have.

Research what your name means. (Look in a baby name book or have an adult help you search the Internet.) Do you think your name describes you accurately? Why or why not?

If you were a boy instead of a girl, or a girl instead of a boy, what name would you choose for yourself?

Would you rather be a baby, a kid, a teenager, or an adult? Why?

All About Me

What makes you angry? What do you do when you are very angry?

How does it feel to be embarrassed? What kinds of things embarrass you?

Tell about something that makes you feel sad.

What makes you feel safe?

What would you like to be when you grow up? Why does this interest you?

All About Me

Describe the funniest or the scariest dream you have ever had.

5

If you could choose one musical instrument to play professionally, which would it be, and why?

Tell about a time when you were teased or left out.

Did you keep the last promise you made to someone? Why or why not?

6

What is the one thing you wish you could do better? Why?

What do you think is the hardest decision you have ever had to make? Were you happy with what you decided?

What would you change about yourself if you could? Why?

What are you most proud of having done in your life so far?

Do you ever feel you have too much to do? Why?

What is the worst accident you have had so far? What happened?

All About Me

What do you think will be the best year of your life? What will happen to make it the best?

Tell about three important events in your life. Put them in order from most important to least important.

Is there something that you have done recently that you are proud of? Tell about it.

What do you think about when you cannot fall asleep at night?

What things were you afraid of a few years ago that no longer bother you?

All About Me

What do you think you will be doing 20̶ years from now?

(handwritten: 10)

What do you think you will look like in 25 years?

Which do you like least—going to the doctor or going to the dentist? Why?

If you could choose, would you rather be able to fly or to become invisible? Why? What other superpower would you like to have?

If you could have a super sense—extra-powerful vision, super hearing, extra-sensitive touch, a stupendously acute sense of taste, or an amazingly keen sense of smell—which would you choose? What would you do with your newly powerful sense?

All About Me

What is your favorite time of day and why?

What is your favorite part about each season of the year?

What is your favorite meal of the day? Why is this your favorite?

If you could have every one of your favorite foods prepared in one meal, what would you request?

If you could eat only one type of fruit and one type of vegetable from now on, which fruit and vegetable would you choose?

All About Me

If you could eat only one type of dessert from now on, what would it be? Which other dessert would be hardest to give up?

If you could drink only one type of drink for the rest of your life, what would it be and why?

When you draw, would you rather draw people, animals, scenery, or something else? Why?

If you had a special thank-you card, whom would you give it to and why?

If you had a choice, would you always take a bath or shower? Why?

All About Me

If you worked at the grocery store, what job would you want to have? Why?

Do you prefer to use crayons, markers, or colorful pencils to color? Explain your choice.

If you could live in a houseboat, in a tepee, or in a mansion, which would you choose? Why is that the best choice of home for you?

If you could spend an hour floating in a hot air balloon, riding a horse, or sailing in a small boat, which would you choose? Why?

If you could go on a trip and take only one thing, what would it be? Why?

16

All About Me

If you could get a new pet, what kind of animal would you choose and why?

If you were on a television show, describe what kind of show it would be.

If you could advertise any product in a commercial, what product would you choose?

If you could choose one sport to play professionally, which would it be and why?

Describe your dream vacation in detail.

  17

All About Me

Would you rather pick what you wear to school or wear a uniform every day?

If you were in charge, what two chores would you choose to do?

If you could be famous when you grow up, what would you want to be famous for?

What is your favorite bedtime story? Who reads it to you?

Are there things that you pretend not to like but really do? Why? Give an example.

All About Me

What are two things that you do not like right now but think you might like in a few years?

If you go to a fair or an amusement park, do you prefer to ride rides, play games, eat food, watch people, or do another activity? Why is that activity your favorite?

Where do you think would be the worst place to be stranded?

Imagine that you are planning your own party. If you have no limits, what would the party be like?

If you had to plan a party for a family member, whom would you choose and what would that person most like to do to celebrate?

All About Me

If you could ask only one question of each new person you meet in your life, what would it be? What will his answer tell you about him?

If you could tell one person that she has influenced your life for the better, who would it be and how did she influence it?

Who is the person you most admire? Why?

If you could meet someone famous, whom would you like to meet and why?

Think about the last promise someone made to you. What was it, and did the person keep it?

© Carson-Dellosa

All About Me

What is the nicest thing you have ever done for someone else?

What is the nicest thing someone else has ever done for you?

What do you do to make other people laugh?

If you could live someone else's life for a week, whose life would you choose and why?

Imagine that you have gone to a sleepover and you are afraid of the dark. Do you ask your friend to leave a light on or do you hide your fear? Explain how you would do either.

All About Me

What furniture would you like to change in your home and why?

Whom do you go to when you have a problem? Why do you choose this person?

Would you rather help someone or be helped? Why? Is it ever hard to ask for help?

What makes you laugh?

Think about a time when you and a friend or family member were planning to do something exciting, but then he had to change or cancel the plans. What happened? How did you react, and how did you feel?

All About Me

When you meet people, what is the first thing you would like for them to know about you?

I would love to have a friend in _____ because . . . .
(country)

Finish that statement. Then, tell what your friend would be like.

If you had to give up all of the things in your bedroom except three, which three things (other than your bed) would you keep? Why?

If you could design the coolest yard or play area for yourself, what would it look like? How big would it be? Draw and write about the yard or area.

If you had no television, computer, or video games, how would your life be different?

All About Me

If you could have any type of bed you want, what would your bed look like and how would it feel to sleep on it?

When you are told to clean your room, what do you do first? What else do you do?

What were your favorite toys to play with in the bathtub? How did you play with them?

If someone gave you money as a gift, how much of it would you spend? How much would you save? How much of it would you give to others?

What is the most important object that you own? Why is it the most important?

All About Me

If you had to choose, would you rather be very tiny, like a mouse, or very large, like an elephant? Why? What do you think it would be like to be a new size?

Imagine that you are an inventor. What would you invent, and how would it change the world?

What was your favorite song when you were very little? Why was it your favorite?

What is the best costume you ever wore? What did you like most about the costume?

If you could add a holiday that everyone in the country would celebrate, what would it be, when would it be, and how would everyone celebrate?

All About Me

What event are you looking forward to right now? What do you think that event will be like?

What fun event or holiday do you feel like you have to wait for the longest? Why?

Where do you feel most comfortable in your home? Why?

If you could borrow a toy from a friend, which toy would you borrow and which friend owns it? Why do you want that toy?

Tell about a gift that you really wanted but were disappointed with after you got it.

All About Me

If you could be a little kid again (age 4 or 5), what toy would you most like to receive as a gift? Why?

Describe the best surprise that has ever been planned for you. It could have been a party, a gift, or even a joke that someone played on you.

If you could buy all new clothes, how would you dress and where would you shop? Why would you choose those clothes?

Pick one character in any book that you have read and explain why you would want to be friends with him.

If you could be any breed of dog, which breed would you be and why?

Family Relationships

If you were in charge of planning Friday night's entertainment for your family, what would you plan?

If you could buy one thing for your family, what would it be and why?

If you could choose your family's dessert tonight, what would it be and why?

Describe someone in your family. What does he look like? What is his personality like?

If you could rename your family members, what names would you give them and why? What name would you give a new sibling?

Family Relationships

What would you do if you woke up in your mom or dad's place? What would your day be like?

Describe what you think your parents' days are like at work. What do they do at their jobs?

With which family member do you have the most in common? Describe the similarities between you and the person. What things do you like to do together?

What one thing does a grown-up in your family say that you wish she wouldn't say? Why?

Other than your parents and siblings, who is your favorite relative? Why?

Family Relationships

If your parents have to punish you for misbehaving, would you prefer to be grounded to your bedroom or have a privilege taken away?

What is one thing that makes your family different from anyone else's?

What do you think would be the hardest part about being a parent?

Do you wish your parents would ask you more or less about how you feel? Why?

What food would you like to make your parents try? Why?

Family Relationships

If you have children of your own, what things will you do differently than your parents? What things will you do the same?

What do you think your parents would wish if they could make two wishes for you?

If your parents were worried about something, would you want them to tell you about it or would you rather not know?

What kinds of things do good parents do?

If you were a parent, what would you do when your child threw a tantrum in the store to get what she wanted?

Family Relationships

What do you think is the one thing that you do that makes your family happy?

If your parents were the children and you were the parent, what household rules would you make? If your parents broke the rules, how would you punish them?

What could you do to make your parents' jobs at home easier?

If you become a parent one day, what one quality would you most like for your children to have? Why? How would you try to encourage this quality?

Describe what you think your parents were like when they were your age.

Family Relationships

What have you learned about cooking from your parents? Do you think that you will be a good cook?

What have you learned about driving from your parents? Do you think that you will be a good driver?

Do you think that it's better to be the youngest, the middle, the oldest, or an only child? Why? Which one are you?

Is it better to have a brother or a sister? Why?

Describe a time when you and your siblings worked together.

Family Relationships

What one thing can always cause you to argue with your brothers and sisters? How could you prevent this argument? What one thing do you and a sibling love to do together?

Name one privilege or advantage you think your sibling gets. Name something you have or can do that your sibling doesn't have or can't do.

Imagine you are an only child. Describe the best thing about living without brothers and sisters. What things would you change?

What is your favorite thing in your grandmother's or grandfather's house?

My everyday life is very different from the way things were when my parents grew up. Do you agree or disagree with this statement? Why?

© Carson-Dellosa

Write What You Think! CD-104228

Family Relationships

If you have grandparents, what do you like best about them?

What does a good grandparent do for a grandchild?

Which family member do you resemble most? Describe the similarities between you and the person. What makes each of you unique?

What is the funniest thing your grandparents have told you about one of your parents? Retell the story.

What would you do if everyone in your family forgot your birthday?

Family Relationships

What one thing do you do that annoys your family the most? Why does it annoy them?

If you had to move and your family let you decide where you should move, where would you want to go? Why?

What is your bedtime? Tell how you feel about it.

What would your life be like if you had 25 brothers and sisters?

What would you change about dinnertime at your house? What would you not change?

© Carson-Dellosa

Friendships

How could you cheer up a sad friend?

Do you think it is harder to say good-bye to a friend who is moving away or hello to (or meet) a new friend who just moved next door?

If your best friend were getting picked on every day at school, what would you say to her to make her feel better? How would you try to help?

How do you make a new friend?

Why do you think your friends are your friends? What makes you a good friend to someone else?

Friendships

How do you know when someone is your very best friend?

If you could teach your friends how to do one thing, what would it be? What makes you a good teacher of that one thing?

If you were asked to tell about your town to a friend who just moved to the area, what would you tell him?

If a friend did something wrong and asked you to keep it a secret, what would you do?

When you invite a friend to your home to play, do you plan activities or just play? If you plan activities, what are they?

38

Friendships

Do you think that there are differences in the kinds of games that boys play with other boys and girls play with other girls? What differences do you see? What similarities do you see?

If you could have anyone as your best friend, who would you choose and why?

Who is the nicest person you know? What is nice about this person?

Think about someone who is special to you. What wish would you make for that person?

What is the best game that you have ever played with a friend?

Friendships

If your friend asks you for help and you feel you already have too much to do, would you help him anyway?

What would you do if your best friend was angry with you?

What would you do if you saw your best friend stealing something? How would it make you feel?

What would you do if you forgot the birthday of a close friend? How would you make it up to her?

Your best friend's parents are thinking about moving. How could you convince them to move to your neighborhood?

School

What is something that has happened at school that your parents would be surprised to learn?

Have you ever daydreamed during school? What did you think about?

What do you remember the most about being in kindergarten?

What has been your favorite part of school this year?

What has been your least favorite part of school this year?

School

If your teacher got sick and couldn't come to school, could your class get its work done without a substitute? Why or why not?

Imagine that you will start going to a new school in the middle of the year. List 10 things that teachers, classmates, and others could do to help you have a good first day.

On the last day of school, your teacher asks you to write a letter to her future students. What are some things you did this year that you would like to tell the new students, and what words of advice do you have?

What is the biggest problem in your classroom right now?

If you could change any school rule, what would it be?

School

If you could do only one after-school activity, what would it be?

If you had to perform in a school talent show, what would your talent be? Describe what your performance would be like.

If you had to design your school's next field trip, where would you go? What would you do to make the field trip fun?

If you were in charge of planning your school's next fund-raiser, what would you do to raise money?

If someone donated one million dollars to your school and you could decide what to do with it, how would you spend it?

School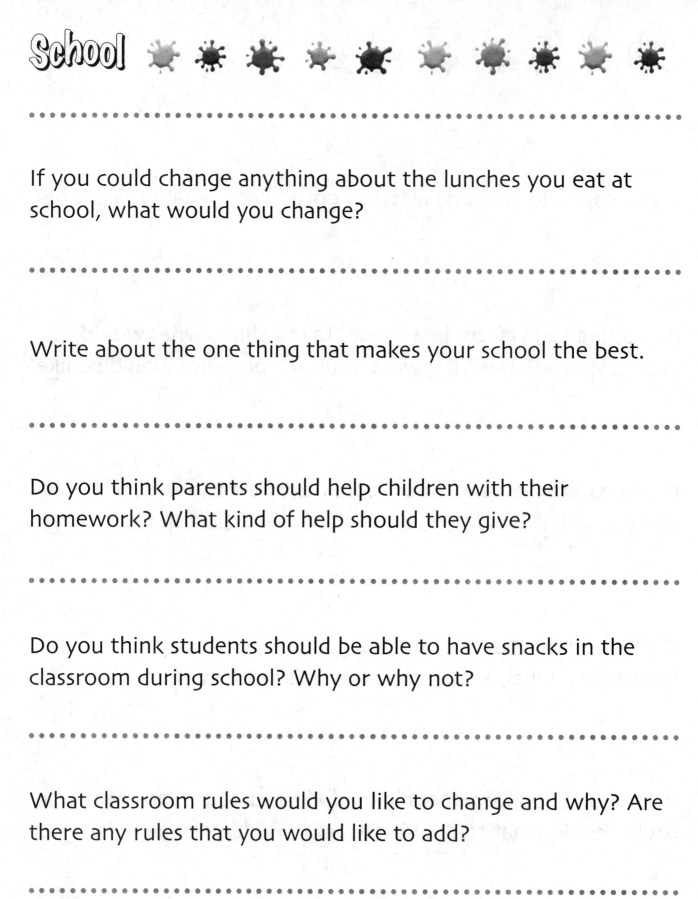

If you could change anything about the lunches you eat at school, what would you change?

Write about the one thing that makes your school the best.

Do you think parents should help children with their homework? What kind of help should they give?

Do you think students should be able to have snacks in the classroom during school? Why or why not?

What classroom rules would you like to change and why? Are there any rules that you would like to add?

School

What is your favorite game to play with your class at recess? Why do you like this game the most?

What is your favorite subject in school and why? Is it the easiest subject for you? What is your least-favorite subject and why?

What topic would you like to learn more about in school? Why?

Would you rather work in a big group, a small group, or by yourself? Why?

Why do you think that some students have a hard time finishing their work?

School

Who do you think has the hardest job at your school and why?

Who do you think has the easiest job at your school and why?

Do you think it is harder to be a student or a teacher? What makes it harder to be the one you chose?

What do you think happens during parent-teacher conferences?

If you were the teacher and your students did not do their homework, what consequences would they have?

School

If you were the teacher, what would you do differently than your teacher?

If you could give your teacher any gift, what would it be and why?

You feel your teacher has acted unfairly toward you. Would you try to talk to her about it? What would you say?

Tell two things that you think teachers want from their students. Why do you think they want these things?

Tell two things that you think students want from their teachers.

School

What do you think your teacher does after leaving school each day?

If you could sit beside anyone in class, whom would you choose and why?

What kinds of things should your teacher do to help you learn?

Do you think that it is better for you to choose your own seat in the classroom or for the teacher to assign seats? Why?

If you could change places with any person in your classroom for just one day, whom would you choose and why?

School

How did you make friends on the first day of school?

If you could have anyone in class come to your house to play, whom would you choose and why?

A trend is something that one or two people start to do and that other people copy. Describe some trends you see in your classroom. Why do you think these are trends?

What do you do when you disagree with a classmate? Do you try to talk about it right away?

Imagine that you have arrived at school early only to find that a classmate is wearing the exact same outfit. What do you do?

49

Academics

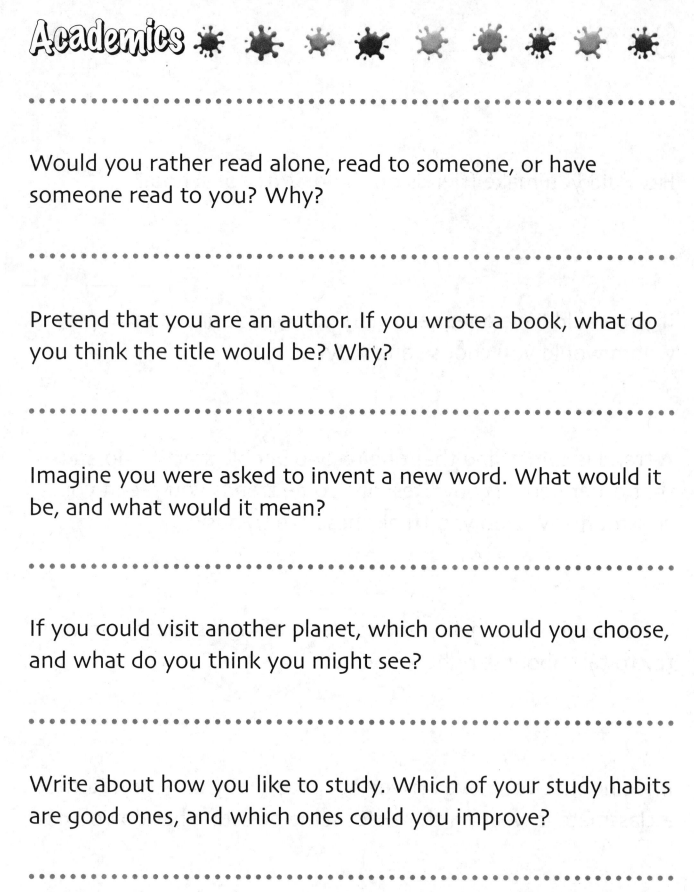

Would you rather read alone, read to someone, or have someone read to you? Why?

Pretend that you are an author. If you wrote a book, what do you think the title would be? Why?

Imagine you were asked to invent a new word. What would it be, and what would it mean?

If you could visit another planet, which one would you choose, and what do you think you might see?

Write about how you like to study. Which of your study habits are good ones, and which ones could you improve?

Academics

Which character from a book that you have read is most like you? How is this character like you?

What is the hardest subject for you in school? Why do you think it is the hardest?

What is the easiest subject for you in school? Why do you think it is the easiest?

What is one talent or skill that you have? How can you turn it into a career?

How do you think school will help you as an adult?

Academics

If you could teach a class in any subject to your friends, what would it be? What makes you a good teacher in that subject?

What school subject do you use most often in your life outside school?

If you could describe the ideal room in which to study and do your homework, what would it be like? How does that differ from where you study now?

In some parts of the world during winter, it is dark for most of the day and night. During summer, it is light for most of the day and night. Would you rather live most of the time in dark or light? Why?

If you had to choose now, what would you like to do when you grow up? What classes are you taking or do you wish you could take to prepare for that job?

Character Education and Safety

Do you act differently when you are with your family or friends than when you are with your teacher? Explain.

If you agreed to sell your bike to a friend and then someone offered you more money, would you still sell the bike to your friend? Why or why not?

How do you feel when you see someone with a disability? Why do you think you feel this way? Should you change your way of thinking?

Some boys and girls choose to be mean to each other. What do you think causes them to be that way?

Have you ever helped someone without her knowing? How did it feel?

How old do you think children should be before they stay home by themselves? Tell why you think that way.

Have you ever picked on someone? How do you think that person felt?

If an older child hit you and told you he would hurt you if you told anyone, what would you do and why?

If you knew it would save the lives of 10 starving children in another country, would you be willing to give up playing with any new toys for the next year?

9|23

If you knew you would not get caught, would you take something that did not belong to you? Why or why not?

Character Education and Safety

What kind of person are you? Describe your character traits. What kind of person do you want to become? Do you think you are on your way to becoming that person? If not, what could you change?

What is the nicest compliment anyone has ever given you?

If you found $5.oo on the floor of your classroom, would you keep it? Why or why not?

You have just heard that there is a huge thunderstorm heading for your house. What would you do to be safe?

What does the word *courage* mean to you? Give an example of someone you think is courageous.

Character Education and Safety

What would you do if someone gave you a gift that you didn't like?

When you ride a school bus, a city bus, or the subway, how should you act?

What would you do if you broke your best friend's toy?

If you could be the best-looking, the most athletic, the smartest, or the nicest student in your class, which would you choose? Why?

10/3/07

If you found some money on the playground, what would you do?

Character Education and Safety

If you could take back one thing you have said, what would it be and why? To whom did you say it?

Is it better to tell a joke that makes everyone except one person laugh and offend that one person, or to not tell any jokes at all?

What makes you jealous?

Is it harder to tell a lie and admit it, or to keep lying for a long time?

Have you ever been blamed for something that you didn't do? Describe how that felt. What was the situation? How did you handle it?

Character Education and Safety

Which is most important to you in a friend: loyalty, generosity, or honesty? Explain why.

What does it mean to have each of these traits: courage, wisdom, humor, and patience? Which one would you most like to have and why?

Your parents have won one million dollars in a lottery. They want to donate $100,000 to a charity. What type of charity should they donate to and why?

Would you read your friend's diary if you found it open?

What is a secret? Do you think it is okay to tell someone's secret? Why or why not?

Character Education and Safety

Your best friend just got a new haircut. You think it looks terrible. What would you say and why?

You are at a friend's house for dinner and are served something that you really dislike. What would you do?

If the class bully apologizes for being mean to you, would you forgive her?

If you made a big mistake at school, would you tell your teacher? What would you do if you made a big mistake at home?

How do you like others to treat you when you make a mistake?

Character Education and Safety

How do you treat others when they make mistakes?

You forgot to do a piece of homework for school because you were busy, and you know your teacher will be disappointed. Your friend offers to let you copy his. What do you do? Why?

Think about the last time you had to say you were sorry for something you said or did. Was it difficult? Why is it hard to apologize sometimes?

Imagine that someone spread a rumor about you through the school. What this person said is untrue. What do you do?

What does it mean to judge someone? Do you judge others more for their actions or more for their meanings? How do you know that you judge people that way?

Character Education and Safety

Do you want to be judged for your meanings or for your actions? What is the difference?

When have you felt like giving up, but didn't, and then succeeded? What does it mean to give up? What does it mean to persevere?

What does the phrase "winners never quit" mean? What do you think the phrase "know when to quit" means?

What would you most like to overhear someone say about you?

Has anyone ever overheard something unkind that you were saying about her? If yes, what did you do? If no, what would you do if that happened?

© Carson-Dellosa

Character Education and Safety

Do you think that entertainers and professional athletes deserve the high salaries they get? Why or why not? What should be the highest-paid professions?

What do you think it means to have good manners? Are manners important? Why or why not?

What would you do if you got lost in a big store?

What would you do if you missed the bus after school?

If you had a new bus driver who got lost on his way to school, what would you do?

Character Education and Safety

A stranger asks you to help her look for her lost puppy. What do you do?

Older children promise to give you $20.00 if you will eat strange things. What do you do?

You see a group of older students scaring little kids and stealing their lunch money. What do you think their punishment should be?

If you and a friend got lost in the woods while hiking, what would you do?

Describe what you should do during a school fire drill.

Points to Ponder/Problem Solving

Tell about something that you could recycle. How would you recycle it?

What do you think the perfect tree house looks like?

Why do you think so many adults drink coffee?

If you were the leader of your country, what would you change about your country?

Which do you think is harder: learning to ride a bike or learning to drive a car? Why?

Points to Ponder/Problem Solving

How would you feel if you could not go to school for a year? What would you do?

If you had permission to look through someone's private possessions, whom would you choose and why?

What makes someone a good writer?

Do you think girls should be allowed to play on boys' soccer teams? Should boys be allowed to play on girls' soccer teams? Why or why not?

Would you rather be a famous movie star or a doctor? Why?

Points to Ponder/Problem Solving

The word *beautiful* means different things to different people. Tell about three things that you think are beautiful.

Do you believe children should be allowed to have every toy that they want? Why or why not?

How old do you think children should be before they are allowed to choose their own bedtimes? Why?

Everyone has problems. What do you think are the two biggest problems of boys and girls who are your age?

How much money do you think a person needs every year to live happily? What should they do with that money?

66

Points to Ponder/Problem Solving

If you could get rid of one thing on Earth, what would it be?

If you could change one thing to make the world a better place, what would it be? Why would you make the change, and who would benefit from it? Why would this change be an important one?

What would happen if people never cooperated (worked together)? Do you think it is important to cooperate? Why or why not?

If you could live in one time period in history, which period would you choose? Why? What do you think your life would be like on a daily basis? (What would you wear? What would you eat? What would you do for fun?)

If you had to either eat the same thing every day or never eat the same thing twice, which would you choose? What food could you eat every day? If you chose the second option, which foods would you never want to try?

  © Carson-Dellosa

Points to Ponder/Problem Solving

How do you know when you are a grown-up?

Many people give pets to children because they say that it will teach responsibility. Do you agree or disagree? Why? If there are pets in your house, who takes care of them?

What is a hero? Do you have to be famous to be a hero? Why or why not?

You have been selected to be the captain of your team at recess. You get to choose your teammates. How do you choose them?

Your class is putting together a time capsule that will be opened in 20 years. What kinds of things do you put in the capsule that tell about your life in the present?

Points to Ponder/Problem Solving

Your new teacher has a disability. He tells you that you can ask him anything about his condition. What are some things that you might ask him?

What makes someone a good artist?

If you could give any gift in the world, what would you give and to whom would you give it?

Would you rather move to a frozen tundra or to a hot desert?

If you could control the weather, what would it be like outside every day? Why?

Points to Ponder/Problem Solving

If you had to get all of the students in your school into one classroom, how would you do it?

Where does lint or dust come from?

What can you learn from having a pet?

How would your life change without electricity and machines like cars? Describe the things in your life that would change and the things that would stay the same. Would life be better or worse? Why?

Describe what you think is inside a cell phone. How do you think it works?

Points to Ponder/Problem Solving

You suddenly have a huge sneeze but don't have any tissues. How do you gracefully take care of your problem?

A magazine editor has asked you to write an article about kids who are your age. What would you write?

If you could import four of the most interesting places in the world into your backyard, what would you choose and why?

What do you think living in a castle would be like? If you had to move to a castle, which would you miss most: television, air conditioning and heat, or indoor plumbing? What else would you miss?

If you could create the world's best magic trick, what would it be? Give directions for performing it and then explain the "trick."

Points to Ponder/Problem Solving

What would make a famous person influential in your life?

What might colors sound like?

If one of the past U.S. presidents could be the principal at your school, whom would you choose and why?

What is the best way to spend a rainy afternoon?

What do you think makes people want to watch the same television shows week after week?

© Carson-Dellosa

Story/Fiction Narrative

What would you do if you woke up with green hair?

What would you do if everything you touched turned to bubble gum?

There's an animal stuck in your tree. What is it, and how did it get there?

In some parts of the world during winter, people build entire hotels, including some of the furniture, out of ice. Write a story about what you think it would be like to spend a few nights there.

Most people like to talk. What would it be like if we could only sing?

Story/Fiction Narrative

Imagine that you and a friend went camping for two days. Tell about your adventure.

You planted a seed, and a magical tree grew. What was hanging from its branches?

What would you do if you could talk to animals? What would you say to them?

Congratulations! You have won a fabulous _____! Tell about how you won it and what you will do with it.

Imagine that you are drinking a soda at a restaurant. When you get to the bottom, you see a bug! Write about what you would do.

Story/Fiction Narrative

If everything in the world had to be just one color, what color would you choose and why? What problems would this cause? What would be good about choosing this color?

If you could snap your fingers and in an instant go anywhere in the world, where would you go, and what would you do there?

Imagine that a crayon company is holding a contest for someone to name the next crayon color that they will make. Tell what you would call it, and describe what it would look like.

Pretend that people on Earth have finally figured out how to live on other planets. Which planet would you most like to live on besides Earth? Why did you choose that planet? You can do some research to help you decide your answer.

You accidentally spill some syrup in the kitchen. You get a sponge, but the more you try to wipe up the syrup, the stickier the floor gets. What do you do to be finally rid of this sticky situation?

Story/Fiction Narrative

If you had to dig a hole to the other side of the earth, how would you do it? Explain what equipment you would need and how long it would take.

Many fairy tales have interesting beginnings. For example, Jack plants magic beans and they grow into a large bean stalk. Choose a fairy tale and, using the same beginning, write a new story about yourself.

Imagine that you are locked in the mall overnight, and the doors to all of the stores are open. What would you do?

A backpack falls out of your locker that is not yours. The contents spill onto the floor. Write a story about what fell out of the bag and how you find the owner.

In a book that you have checked out from the library, you find a mysterious note. What is the note about, and who wrote it?

© Carson-Dellosa

Story/Fiction Narrative

You have invented a new kind of candy. List its ingredients and how to make it. Are any of the ingredients "secret"?

One day, your teacher decides that no one in her class is allowed to wear shoes any longer, only socks. What would that be like?

Your little brother or sister has been chosen to live in another country. Write a story about how this affects your family.

One day, you find some flowers that you have never seen before. You take one home and try to find out what kind it is but can't find any information. It is an undiscovered species. Tell how this changes your life.

You have been offered a round trip ride in a time machine and can travel any distance into the past. Where would you want to go? Describe the trip.

© Carson-Dellosa

Story/Fiction Narrative

While watching the news, you learn that your community has been selected as "community of the year." Write a story about what your community does to celebrate.

When you go to your mailbox one day, you find a treasure map with a letter addressed to you. Write a story about the letter and map. Who sent the letter? If you look for the treasure, do you find it? If you find it, what is it?

Think about your two favorite television shows. Imagine that you are in charge of making a new show that combines all of the characters in your two favorites. Write about what would happen in the first episode of your new show.

You wake up one morning to find that you are no longer a student. You are the new teacher of your class! No one recognizes who you really are, and you have to teach the class. Write a story about what happens.

You find out that your principal is really a superhero! Write a story about how you find this out and what the principal uses his superpowers for.

Story/Fiction Narrative

You have been given the task of adding one month to the year. What would you call it? When would it happen? What would we celebrate during that month?

One morning you wake up to find that your hands and feet have switched places. Describe what happens that day.

You hear a faint sound coming from your hand. You realize that the sound is coming from under your fingernails. Do you cut your nails or become friends with the creatures living under them? Describe what happens.

One morning you wake up to find that you are taller than most basketball players. Describe what happens as you try to get ready for school.

A piece of your headphones slides into your ear canal. Now as you walk around, you pick up various signals. What do you hear—anything secret or mysterious? What do you do?

Story/Fiction Narrative

Would you prefer to live underwater or in the trees? How would your life be different?

What kind of plant would you like to be? Write a story about what your life would be like as that plant.

You find two dogs and a cat huddled near your home. Write a story about their adventures.

You wake up one morning to discover that your school has vanished; there is just an empty field where it used to be. What happened?

A family member discovers that every time he puts on a certain hat, he has a strong urge to play basketball. Then, when he plays he never misses a shot, even from the other end of the court. What does he do with this knowledge?

© Carson-Dellosa